Christmas Stitchin'

by Anne Van Wagner Young

Leisure Arts Inc. • Maumelle Arkansas

TABLE OF CONTENTS

While some finishing products may no longer be available, these versatile designs can be used in a myriad of oh-so creative ways.

Cover items made and patterns tested by Susan Barrs, Liz Berger, DiAnne Drennan, Joyce Fisher, Susan Foster, Nell Harris, Mary Reese Hicks, Susan James, Nan Laux, Joan Nadler, Ray Ellen Odle, Patricia O'Meara, Julia Penaloza, Barbara Penney, Linda Webb, and Joan Wood.

Made in U.S.A.

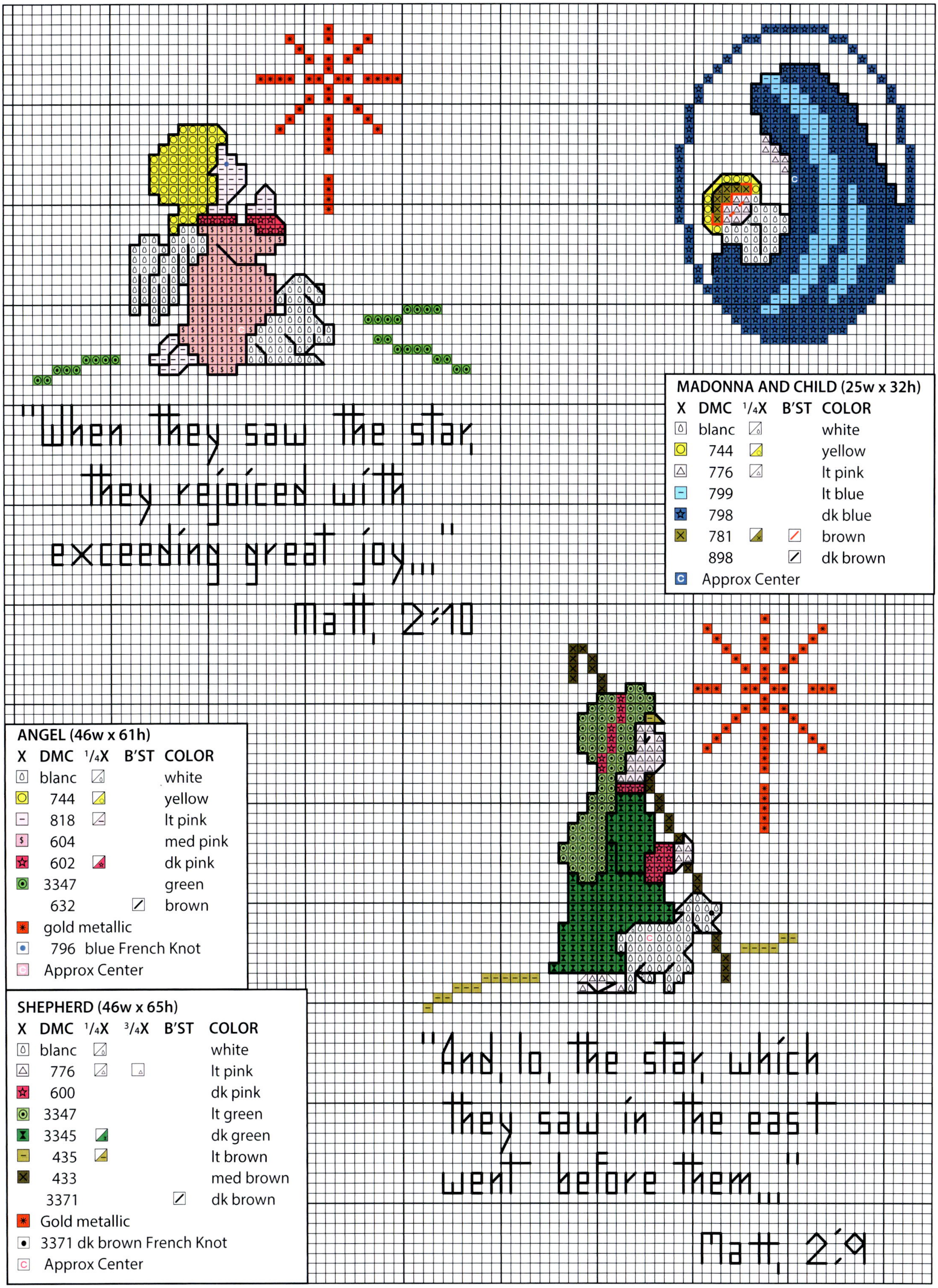

MADONNA AND CHILD (25w x 32h)

X	DMC	1/4X	B'ST	COLOR
✓	blanc	✓		white
✓	744	✓		yellow
✓	776	✓		lt pink
✓	799			lt blue
✓	798			dk blue
✓	781	✓	✓	brown
	898		✓	dk brown

C Approx Center

ANGEL (46w x 61h)

X	DMC	1/4X	B'ST	COLOR
✓	blanc	✓		white
✓	744	✓		yellow
✓	818	✓		lt pink
✓	604			med pink
✓	602	✓		dk pink
✓	3347			green
	632		✓	brown

gold metallic

796 blue French Knot

C Approx Center

SHEPHERD (46w x 65h)

X	DMC	1/4X	3/4X	B'ST	COLOR
✓	blanc	✓			white
✓	776	✓	✓		lt pink
✓	600				dk pink
✓	3347				lt green
✓	3345	✓			dk green
✓	435	✓			lt brown
✓	433				med brown
	3371			✓	dk brown

Gold metallic

3371 dk brown French Knot

C Approx Center

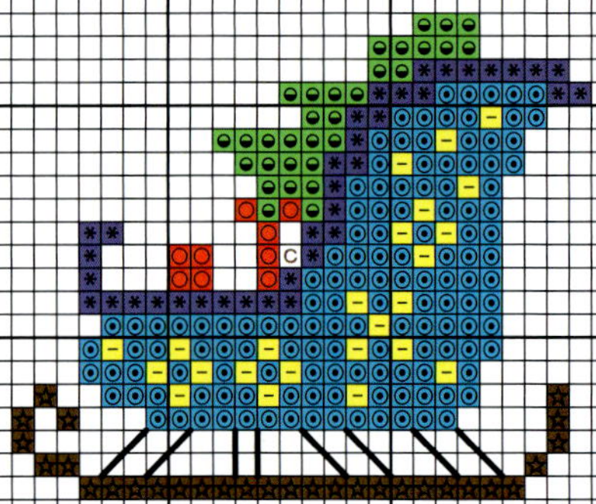

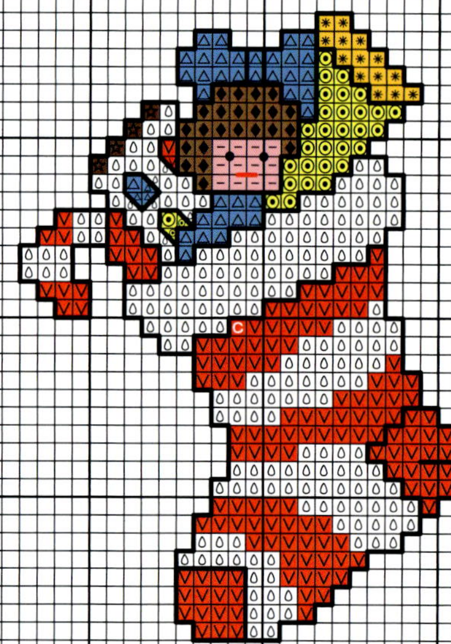

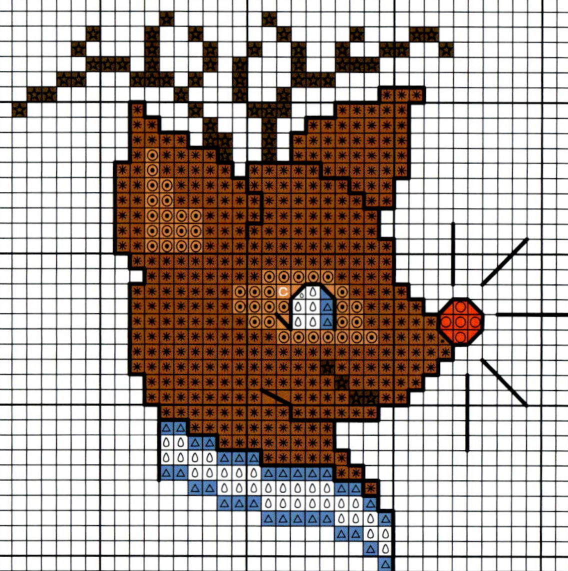

SLEIGH (26w x 21h)

X	DMC	B'ST	COLOR
−	725		yellow
O	321		red
⊙	996		lt blue
∗	995		med blue
●	699		green
★	3371	/	dk brown
C	Approx Center		

REINDEER (38 w x 37h)

X	DMC	1/4X	B'ST	COLOR
◊	blanc	◺		white
O	666	◺		red
△	995	◺		blue
⊙	402	◺		lt rust
∗	921	◺		med rust
★	3371		/	dk brown
C	Approx Center			

STOCKING (25w x 35h)

X	DMC	1/4X	B'ST	COLOR
◊	blanc	◺		white
⊙	725	◺		yellow
∗	783			gold
−	776			pink
V	666	◺	/	red
△	996	◺		blue
◆	435			brown
★	3371		/	dk brown
•	996 blue French Knot			
C	Approx Center			

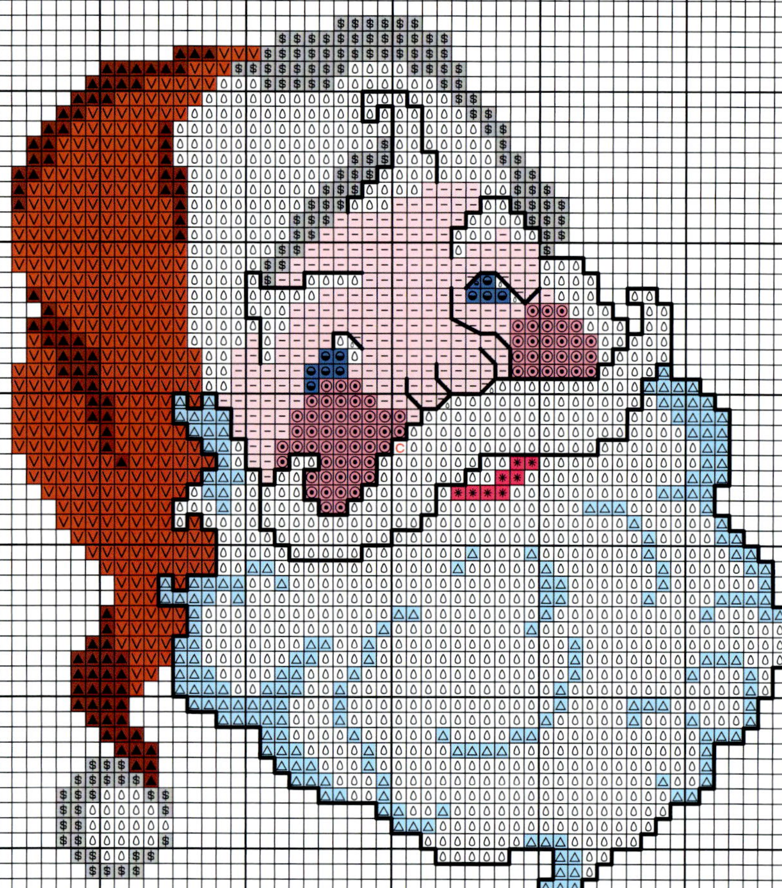

SANTA #1 (53w x 58h)

X	DMC	1/4X	B'ST	COLOR
◊	blanc	◺		white
−	818	◺		lt pink
⊙	776			med pink
∗	962			dk pink
V	666			red
▲	817			dk red
△	828			lt blue
●	791	◺		dk blue
$	762			lt grey
	3371		/	dk brown
C	Approx Center			

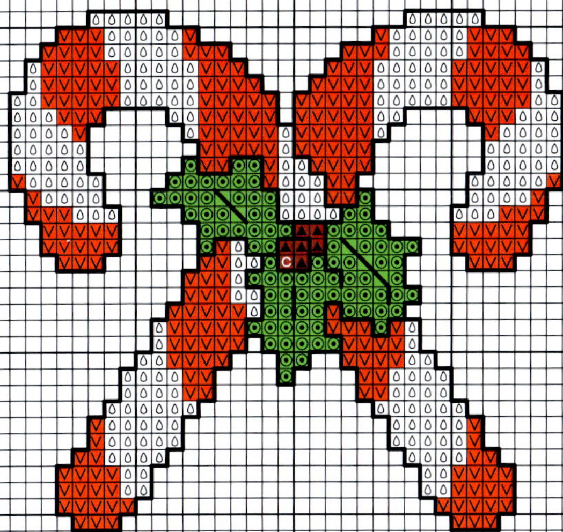

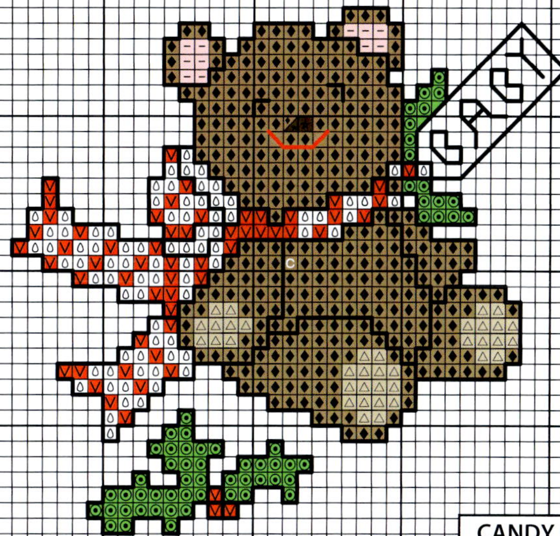

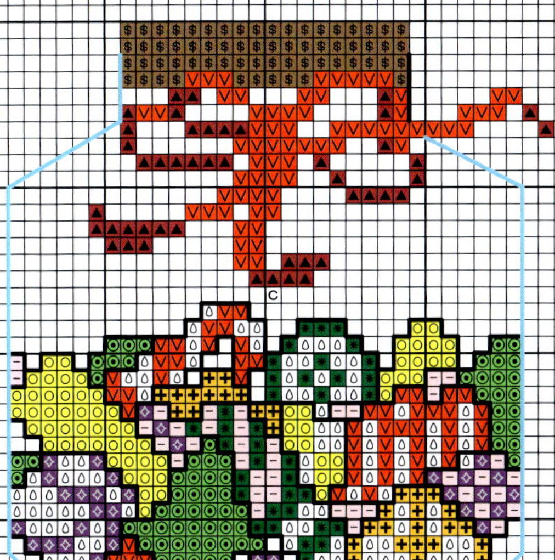

CANDY CANES (35w x 32h)

X	DMC	B'ST	COLOR
	blanc		white
	666		red
	321		dk red
	704		green
	3371	/	dk brown
C	Approx Center		

CANDY JAR (34w x 33h)

X	DMC	B'ST	COLOR
	blanc		white
	725		yellow
	608		orange
	776		pink
	666		red
	321		dk red
	718		purple
	796	/	blue
	704		lt green
	700		med green
$	435		lt brown
	3371	/	dk brown
C	Approx Center		

HOLLY WREATH (38w x 41h)

X	DMC	B'ST	COLOR
	666		red
	321		dk red
	704		lt green
	3371	/	dk brown
	321		dk red Smyrna Cross
C	Approx Center		

TEDDY BEAR (37w x 34h)

X	DMC	1/4X	3/4X	B'ST	COLOR
	blanc				white
	776				pink
	666			/	red
	701	◪			green
	402				lt tan
	921	◪			med tan
	3371		◪	/	dk brown
C	Approx Center				

LARGE BLUE BELLS (30w x 32h)

X	DMC	¼X	B'ST	COLOR
	725			yellow
	783			gold
	666			red
	321			dk red
	996			lt blue
	995			dk blue
	704			green
	3371			brown

C Approx Center

SANTA CLAUS #2 (27w x 24h)

C Approx Center

MRS. CLAUS (23w x 23h)

C Approx Center

X	DMC	¼X	B'ST	COLOR
	blanc			white
	776			lt pink
	666			red
	826			blue
	701			green
	3371			brown
	415			grey

TRAIN (44w x 32h)

X	DMC	¼X	B'ST	COLOR
	725			yellow
	776			pink
	666			red
	796			blue
	704			green
	762			lt grey
	414			dk grey
	435			brown
	898			dk brown
	796			blue French Knot

C Approx Center

PUMP (43w x 52h)

X	DMC	¼X	B'ST	COLOR
	blanc			white
	726			yellow
	666			red
	321			dk red
	828			lt blue
	648			lt taupe
	3022			med taupe
	645			dk taupe
	976			dk gold
	436			lt brown
	434			med brown
	3371			dk brown
	415			lt grey
	321			dk red French Knot

C Approx Center

SANTA TRIMMING TREE (27w x 23h)

X	DMC	B'ST	COLOR
	blanc		white
	725		yellow
	776		pink
	666		red
	996		lt blue
	700		green
	898		brown
	3371		dk brown
	796 med blue French Knot		
	Approx Center		

LARGE CANDLE WITH HOLLY (31w x 35h)

X	DMC	1/4X	B'ST	COLOR
	725			yellow
	783			dk gold
	608			orange
	666			red
	321			dk red
	701			med green
	699			dk green
	3371			dk brown
	Approx Center			

SNOWMEN CAROLERS (35w x 35h)

X	DMC	1/4X	B'ST	COLOR
	blanc			white
	783			gold
	666			red
	996			lt blue
	995			dk blue
	704			lt green
	701			dk green
	414			med grey
	898			dk brown
	Approx Center			

MAILBOX (44w x 51h)

X	DMC	1/4X	3/4X	B'ST	COLOR
	blanc				white
	321				dk red
	3325				blue
	502				blue green
	704				lt green
	699				dk green
	402				lt rust
	920				dk rust
	436				vy lt brown
	434				lt brown
	840				med brown
	801				dk brown
	3371				vy dk brown
	415				lt grey
	414				med grey
	321 dk red French Knot				
	3371 vy dk brown French Knot				
	Approx Center				

ADE
MERRY CHRISTMAS

Season's
Greetings
1981
EKL
HOLIDAY
GREETINGS

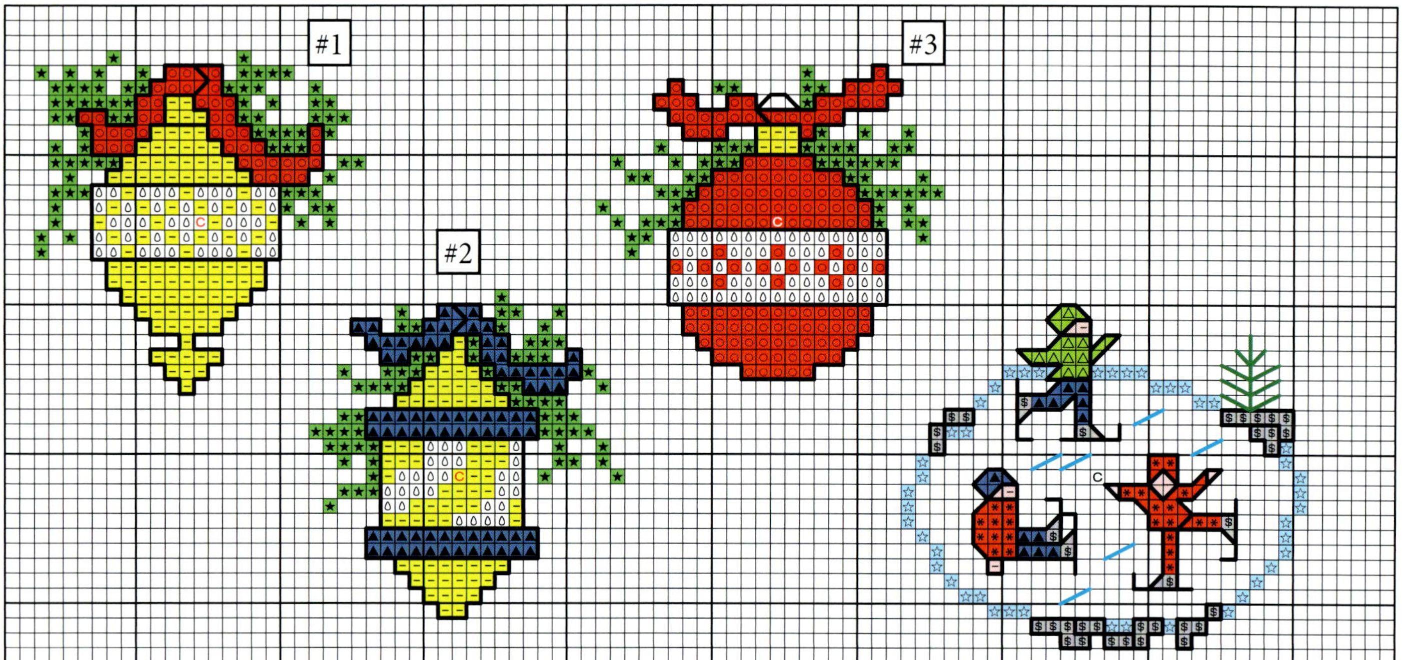

OLD FASHIONED ORNAMENTS

#1 (23w x 23h) — C Approx Center
#2 (22w x 22h) — C Approx Center
#3 (23w x 21h) — C Approx Center

X	DMC	B'ST	COLOR
◊	725		white
▬	783		yellow
○	666		red
▲	321		blue
★	701		green
	3371	⁄	dk brown

CHILDREN SKATING (28w x 23h)

X	DMC	1/4X	B'ST	COLOR
▬	776	◩		lt pink
✱	666	◩		red
☆	3325	◩	⁄	lt blue
▲	312	◩		dk blue
△	704	◩		lt green
	699		⁄	dk green
	3371		⁄	dk brown
$	318	◩		grey

C Approx Center

WAITING FOR SANTA (45w x 76h)

X	DMC	1/4X	3/4X	B'ST	COLOR
◊	blanc	◩			white
▬	725	◩			yellow
○	776	◩			lt pink
✱	666				red
✕	996	◩			blue
△	701				lt green
◒	699				dk green
✚	402	◩	◩		lt tan
	921			⁄	dk tan
☆	435	◩		⁄	med brown
	3371			⁄	dk brown
◈	762	◩			lt grey
★	318			⁄	med grey
$	414				dk grey

C Approx Center

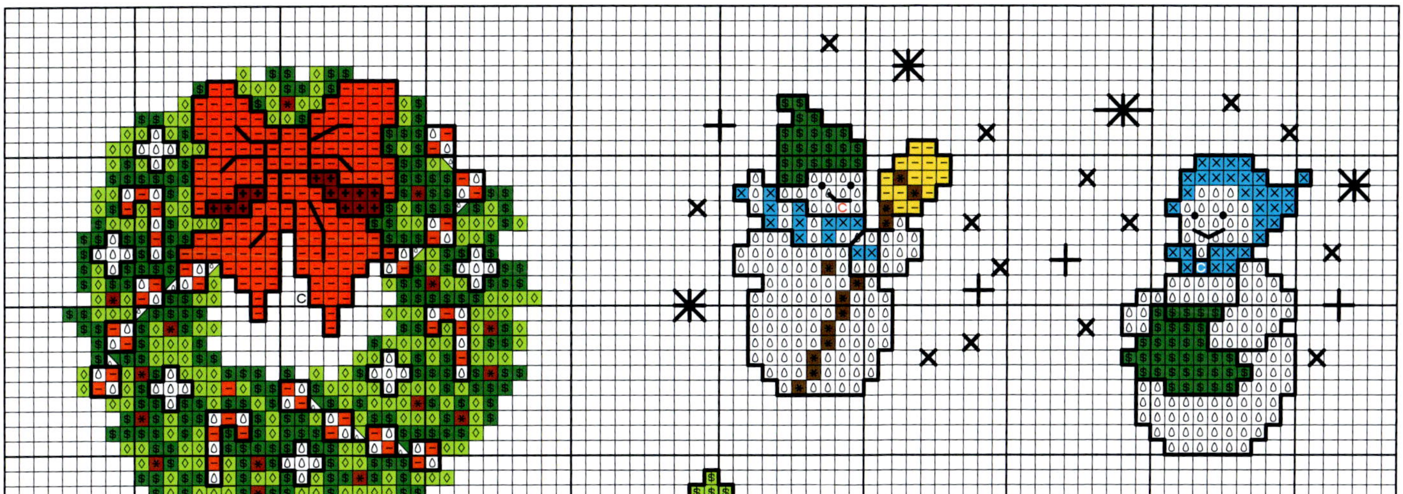

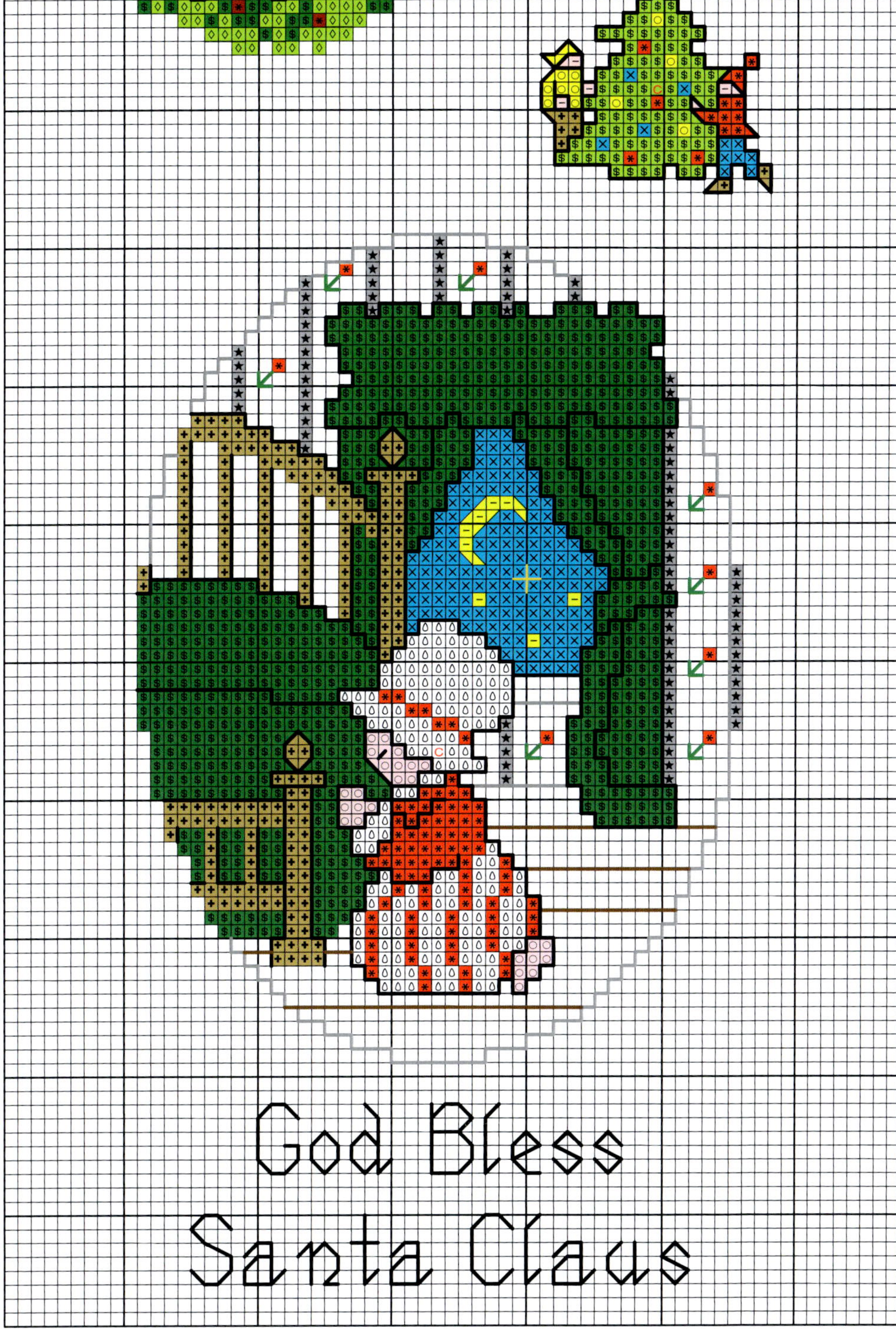

CANDY WREATH (33w x 32h)

X	DMC	¹/₄X	³/₄X	B'ST	COLOR
	blanc		✓		white
	666				red
	321				dk red
	702	✓			med green
	909	✓			dk green
	3371			✓	dk brown
	666 red Smyrna Cross				
	Approx Center				

MR. SNOWMAN (23w x 24h)

Approx Center

MRS. SNOWMAN (22w x 24h)

Approx Center

X	DMC	B'ST	COLOR
	blanc	✓*	white
	783		gold
	996		blue
	704		green
	3371	✓**	dk brown
	3371 dk brown French Knot		

*Snowflakes **Mr. and Mrs. Snowman

CHILDREN TRIMMING TREE (17w x 15h)

X	DMC	¹/₄X	B'ST	COLOR
	725	✓		yellow
	776	✓		lt pink
	666	✓		red
	312			dk blue
	704	✓		lt green
	435	✓		brown
	3371		✓	dk brown
	Approx Center			

GOD BLESS SANTA CLAUS (45w x 76h)

X	DMC	¹/₄X	³/₄X	B'ST	COLOR
	blanc				white
	445		✓	✓	yellow
	725	✓			dk yellow
	776	✓			pink
	666				red
	825	✓			blue
	704	✓		✓	green
	435			✓	brown
	3371			✓	dk brown
	318			✓	grey
	Approx Center				

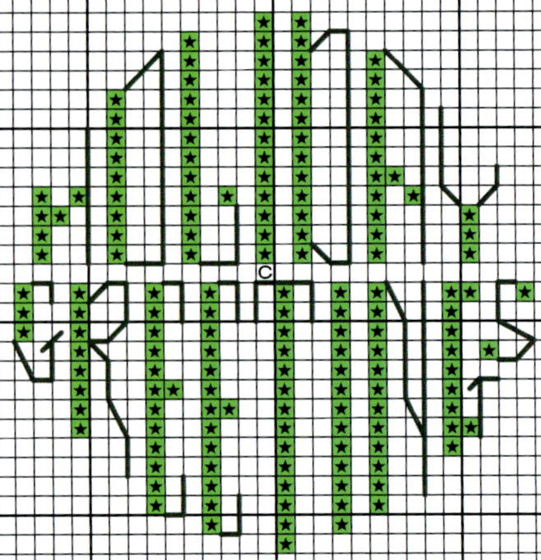

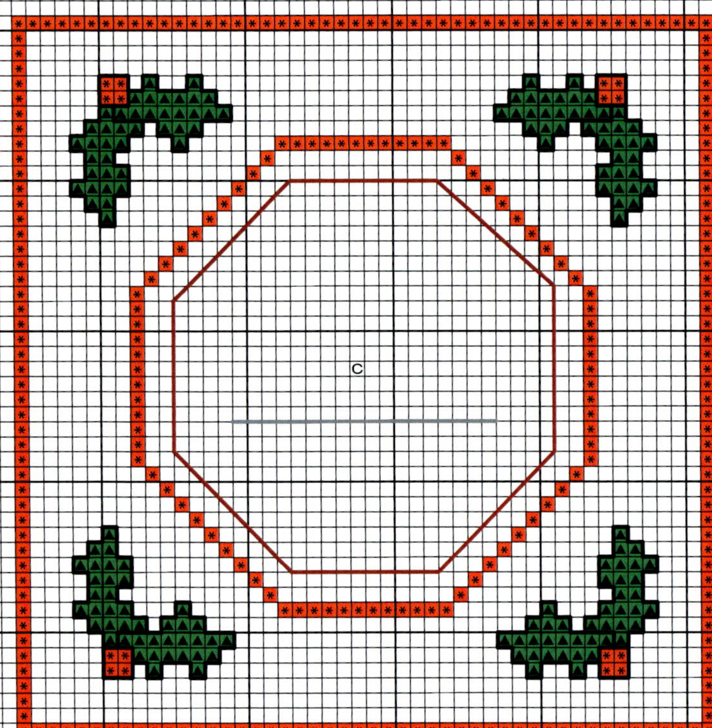

HOLIDAY GREETINGS (28w x 28h)

X	DMC	B'ST	COLOR
★	699	⁄	dk green

C Approx Center

MERRY CHRISTMAS (48w x 48h)

X	DMC	3/4X	B'ST	COLOR
*	666	◢	⁄	red

C Approx Center

INITIAL ROUND DESIGN (34w x 36h)

X	DMC	B'ST	COLOR
△	725		yellow
*	666		red
–	701		lt green
★	699		dk green
	3371	⁄	dk brown

C Approx Center

— grey line - initial placement

INITIAL SQUARE DESIGN (48w x 48h)

X	DMC	B'ST	COLOR
*	666	⁄	red
▲	909		green
	3371	⁄	dk brown

C Approx Center

— grey line - initial placement

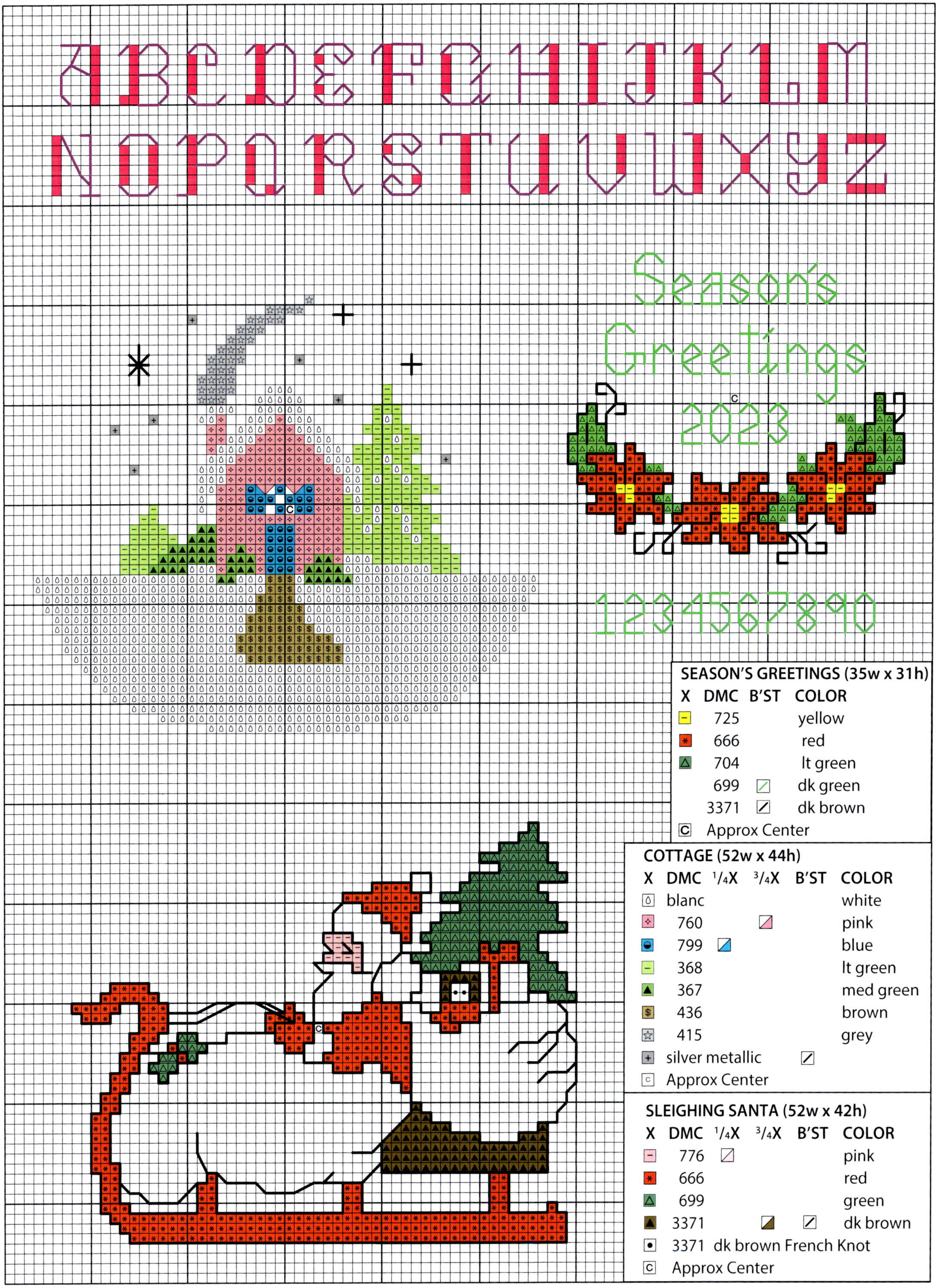

SEASON'S GREETINGS (35w x 31h)

X	DMC	B'ST	COLOR
–	725		yellow
*	666		red
△	704		lt green
	699	/	dk green
	3371	/	dk brown
C	Approx Center		

COTTAGE (52w x 44h)

X	DMC	1/4X	3/4X	B'ST	COLOR
◊	blanc				white
✧	760		/		pink
◒	799	/			blue
–	368				lt green
▲	367				med green
$	436				brown
☆	415				grey
+	silver metallic			/	
C	Approx Center				

SLEIGHING SANTA (52w x 42h)

X	DMC	1/4X	3/4X	B'ST	COLOR
–	776	/			pink
*	666				red
△	699				green
▲	3371		/	/	dk brown
•	3371 dk brown French Knot				
C	Approx Center				

Approx Center

SNOWFLAKE #1 (15w x 15h)
SMALL WREATH (15w x 15h)
SNOWFLAKE #2 (17w x 17h)
SMALL CANDLE (21w x 21h)
CHRISTMAS TREE (9w x 10h)
SMALL GOLD BELLS (19w x 18h)

X	DMC	B'ST	COLOR
	blanc		white
	725		yellow
	783		med gold
	608		orange
	666		red
	826		lt blue
	704		lt green
	701		med green
	699		dk green
	3371		dk brown

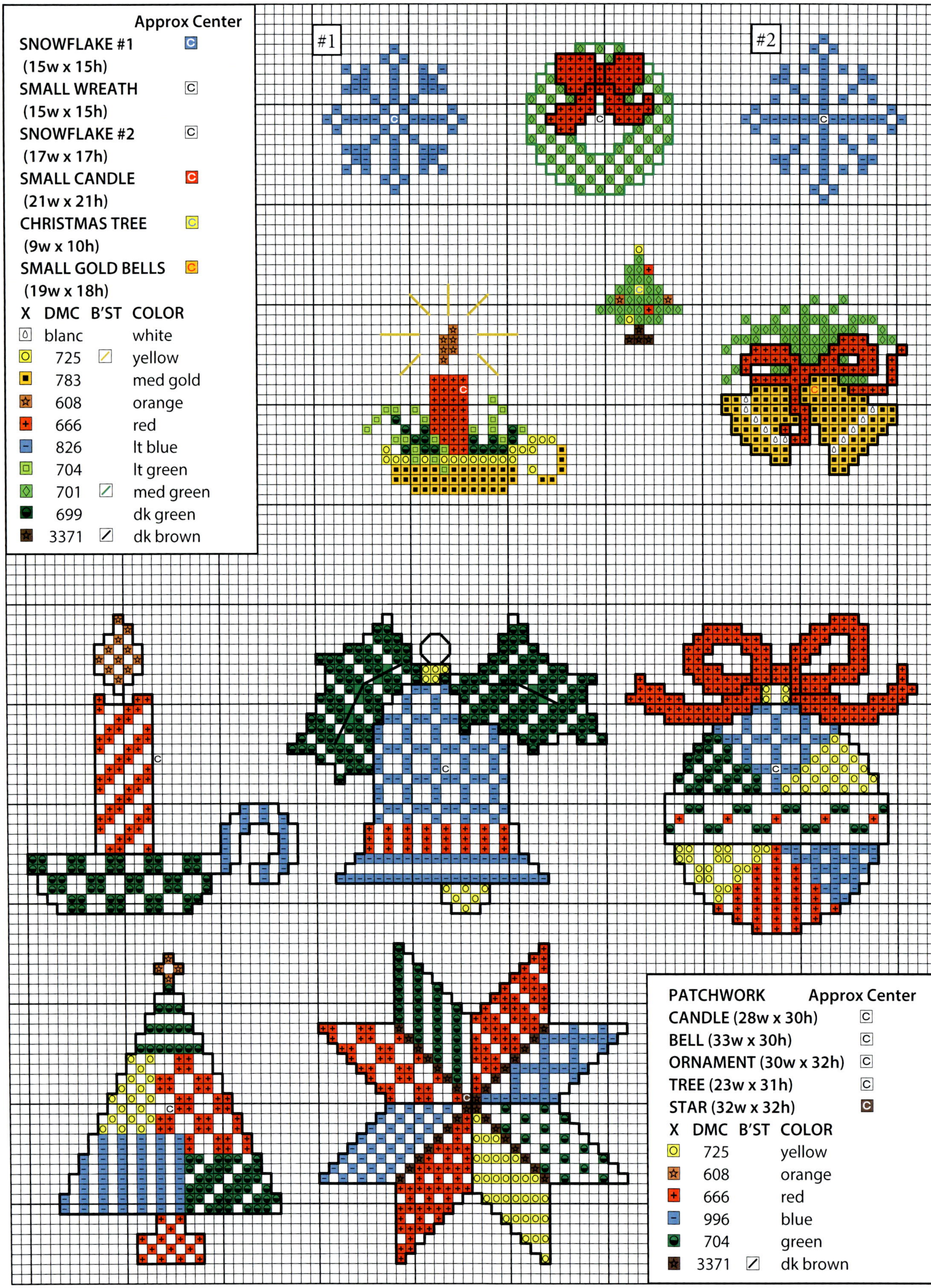

PATCHWORK Approx Center

CANDLE (28w x 30h)
BELL (33w x 30h)
ORNAMENT (30w x 32h)
TREE (23w x 31h)
STAR (32w x 32h)

X	DMC	B'ST	COLOR
	725		yellow
	608		orange
	666		red
	996		blue
	704		green
	3371		dk brown

GENERAL INSTRUCTIONS

WORKING WITH CHARTS

How To Read Charts: Each of the designs is shown in chart form. Each square on the chart represents one needlework stitch. Each square is shown in color, and in most cases, also with a symbol. This method of charting with color enables you to see approximately what the design will look like. By giving you a symbol also, the guesswork of determining shading is eliminated. The straight lines on the chart indicate Backstitching. These lines are shown either in color or black; the color to use is indicated on the color key.

How To Compute Finished Sizes: While the number of stitches varies with each charted design, the finished size of your needlework depends upon the **thread count per inch** of the fabric being used. To compute the size of fabric needed: Divide the number of squares (stitches) across the width or length of the chart by the thread count of your fabric. For example: 80 squares horizontally on the chart worked on Aida 14 will yield a design 5¾" wide. Repeat for vertical stitch count. Then add the amount of background you want plus a generous margin for finishing.

To Use the Table: Find the approximate number of stitches vertically or horizontally in the left hand column. Follow the line across to the column for your fabric thread count. The figure is the size your stitched piece will be.

NUMBER OF STITCHES IN DESIGN (Width or Height) \ THREADS PER INCH OF FABRIC	11	14	18	22
10	7/8	3/4	1/2	1/2
20	1 7/8	1 3/8	1 1/8	7/8
30	2 3/4	2 1/8	1 5/8	1 3/8
40	3 5/8	2 7/8	2 1/4	1 7/8
50	4 1/2	3 5/8	2 3/4	2 1/4
60	5 1/2	4 1/4	3 3/8	2 3/4
70	6 3/8	5	3 7/8	3 1/8
80	7 1/4	5 3/4	4 1/2	3 5/8
90	8 1/8	6 3/8	5	4 1/8
100	9 1/8	7 1/8	5 1/2	4 1/2

Basic Thread Counts

Aida: 11, 14 and 18 per inch

Hardanger: 22 per inch (sometimes worked over 2 threads in which case 11 per inch)

If working on an unlabeled canvas or fabric, measure and count the number of threads that fall within an inch.

Where To Start: The approximate center of each chart has been marked with a "c". You may start at any point, but be sure to allow plenty of margin. It is better to waste a little fabric than to come up short after hours of stitching!

Recommended Colors: We refer to all colors by name and also by DMC embroidery floss numbers.

STITCHING TIPS

Preparing Fabric: Overcast raw edges of fabric. Locate horizontal and vertical centers by folding your fabric in half, top to bottom and again right to left.

Preparing Thread: When working with stranded threads, separate, then realign them before threading needle. This gives a smoother stitch. For ease in stitching, you may thread a needle with each color to be used; lead thread away from working area and anchor needle in top of work until color is required again. Keep stitching tension consistent. Begin and end working threads by running under several stitches on back; never tie knots.

Number Of Strands: The table below shows the recommended number of strands to use when working with stranded cotton/floss and needle sizes.

Fabric	Strands	Needle Size
Aida 11 or Hardanger over 2	2-3 strands for cross stitch; 2-3 strands for Backstitch	24
Aida 14 Fiddlers Cloth	2 strands for cross stitch; 1-2 strands for backstitch	24
Aida 18, Davos or Floba	1-2 strands for cross stitch; 1-2 strands for backstitch	24-26
Hardanger 22	1 strand for cross stitch; 1-2 strands for backstitch	26

Counted Cross Stitch Projects: Work one cross stitch to correspond to each square on the chart. For horizontal rows, work stitches in two journeys *(Fig. 1)*. For vertical rows, complete each stitch as shown *(Fig. 2)*. When working on Hardanger over 2 threads, work cross stitch as in **Fig. 3**.

Fig. 1

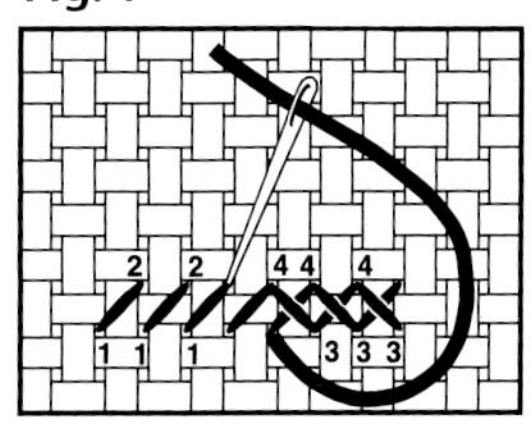

Fig. 2

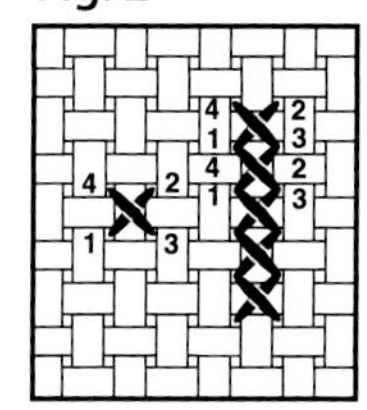

Fig. 3

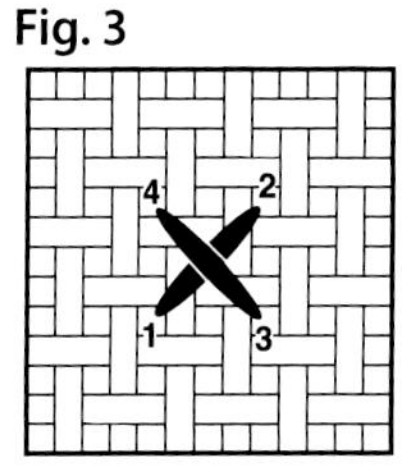

One-Quarter Stitch and Three-Quarter Stitch (1/4X and 3/4X): Stitch 1-2 is the One-Quarter Stitch (1/4X) *(Fig. 4)*. Stitch 3-4 is a Three-Quarter Stitch (3/4X). It may be worked in the same color or contrasting color floss. **Fig. 5** shows this technique when working over two fabric threads.

Fig. 4

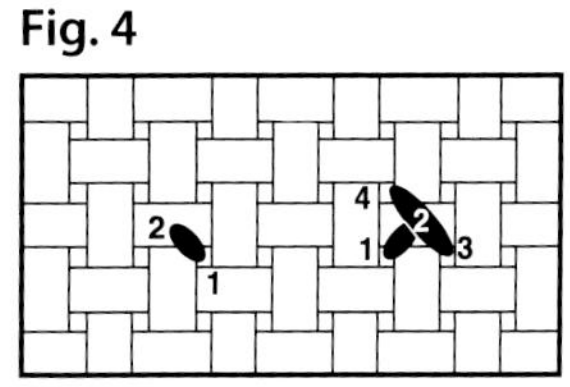

Fig. 5

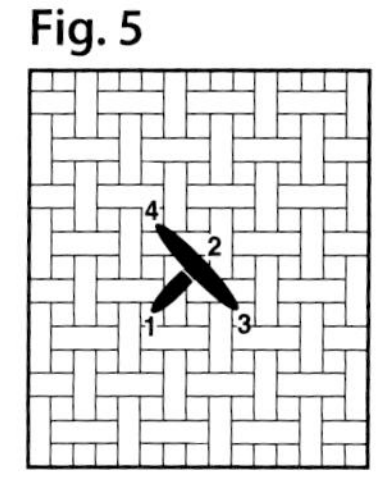

Backstitching: Outline detail (shown on chart and on color key by black or colored straight lines) should be worked by Backstitching *(Fig. 6)* after the design has been completed. Backstitch for Hardanger over 2 threads is shown in **Fig. 7**.

Fig. 6

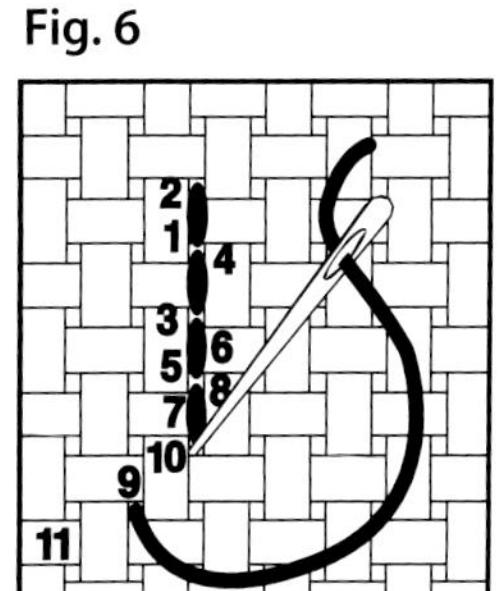

Fig. 7

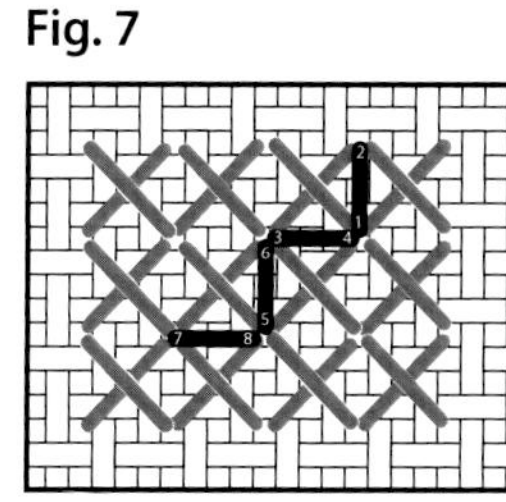

Smyrna Cross Stitch: Stitches 1-4 are the cross stitch. Stitches 5-8 are then worked on top of the completed cross stitch ***(Fig. 8)***.

Fig. 8

French Knot: Bring yarn up at 1. Wrap yarn once around needle and insert needle at 2, holding end of yarn with non-stitching fingers ***(Fig. 9)***. Tighten knot, then pull needle through fabric holding yarn until it must be released. For a larger knot, use more strands; wrap only once.

Fig. 9

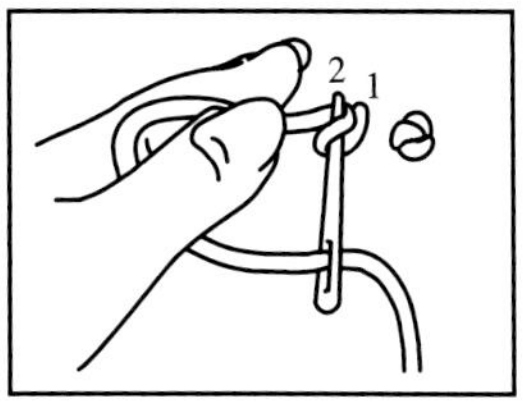

FINISHING

Canning Jar Lid Finishing

Using lid as pattern, cut 1 circle from thin cardboard. From lining fabric, cut circle $^{1}/_{2}$" larger on all sides than lid. Cover circle with lining fabric and glue edges to back to form lining piece. Put small amount of fiber fill on top of lid, center cross stitch on top. Place ring over fabric so that design "puffs". Trim edges to $^{1}/_{2}$" and glue to back of lid. Glue lining piece to inside of ring and to back of lid. Place on jar. Thread $^{1}/_{4}$" ribbon through eyelet beading and glue to edge of ring.

Button Ornament Finishing

Center design on fabric. Cover two $1^{7}/_{8}$" buttons following instructions in purchased kit. Pay careful attention that design is centered on button shell. Bend button shanks to one side. Glue buttons together by applying a small amount of white glue to back edge of one button and holding firmly in place until glue sets. Place $^{1}/_{4}$" ribbon over seam and tie in a bow at top. Fasten nylon line to ornament at bow. Knot line tightly 3" from ornament and trim excess ends.

PROJECTS

Angel: Ivory Aida 14 - $3^{3}/_{8}$" x $4^{3}/_{8}$". Inserted in 5" x 7" frame.
Shepherd: Ivory Aida 14 - $3^{3}/_{8}$" x $4^{3}/_{4}$". Inserted in 5" x 7" frame.
Patchwork Tree: Ivory Aida 14 - $1^{5}/_{8}$" x $2^{1}/_{4}$". Inserted in 3" ring.
Patchwork Candle: Ivory Aida 18 - $1^{5}/_{8}$" x $1^{3}/_{4}$". Inserted in 3" ring.
Patchwork Star: Ivory Hardanger - $1^{1}/_{2}$" x $1^{1}/_{2}$". Inserted in lucite napkin ring. Also Ivory Aida 18 - $1^{7}/_{8}$" x $1^{7}/_{8}$". Inserted in $2^{1}/_{2}$" square frame.
Patchwork Ornament: Ivory Hardanger - $1^{3}/_{8}$" x $1^{1}/_{2}$". Inserted in $2^{1}/_{2}$" ring.
Patchwork Bell: Ivory Hardanger - $1^{1}/_{2}$" x $1^{3}/_{8}$". Inserted in lucite napkin ring. Also Ivory Aida 14 - $2^{3}/_{8}$" x $2^{1}/_{4}$". Inserted in 3" ring.
Cottage: Dk Blue Hardanger - $2^{3}/_{8}$" x 2". Inserted in $2\frac{1}{2}$" ring.
Children Trimming Tree: Ivory Aida 14 - $1^{1}/_{4}$" x $1^{1}/_{8}$". Inserted in $2^{1}/_{2}$" ring.
Children Skating: Ivory Aida 14 - 2" x $1^{5}/_{8}$". Inserted in $2^{1}/_{2}$" ring.
Sleighing Santa: Ivory Hardanger - $2^{3}/_{8}$" x 2". Inserted in 3" ring. Also Ivory Aida 14 - $3^{3}/_{4}$" x 3". Inserted in lucite napkin/card caddy.
Small Candle: Ivory Aida 18 - $1^{1}/_{8}$" x $1^{1}/_{8}$". Inserted in $1^{3}/_{4}$" ring.
Mrs. Snowman: Red Aida 14 - $1^{5}/_{8}$" x $1^{3}/_{4}$". Inserted in $2\frac{1}{2}$" ring.
Mr. Snowman: Red Aida 14 - $1^{5}/_{8}$" x $1^{3}/_{4}$". Inserted in $2^{1}/_{2}$" ring.
Santa Claus #1: Dk Blue Hardanger - $2^{1}/_{2}$" x $2^{3}/_{4}$". Inserted in oval frame. Also Ivory Aida 14 - $3^{7}/_{8}$" x $4^{1}/_{4}$". Inserted in 5" x 7" frame.
Season's Greetings: Ivory Hardanger - $1^{5}/_{8}$" x $1^{1}/_{2}$". Inserted in $2^{1}/_{2}$" square frame. Also Ivory Hardanger - For finishing, refer to Canning Jar Lid Finishing.
Sleigh: Ivory Hardanger - $1^{1}/_{4}$" x 1". For finishing, refer to Button Ornament Finishing. Also stitched on Hardanger - Inserted in wooden ornament.
Old Fashioned Ornament #1: Ivory Aida 14 - $1^{5}/_{8}$" x $1^{5}/_{8}$". Inserted in $2^{1}/_{2}$" ring.
Old Fashioned Ornament #2: Ivory Aida 14 - $1^{5}/_{8}$" x $1^{5}/_{8}$". Inserted in $2^{1}/_{2}$" ring.
Old Fashioned Ornament #3: Lt Blue Aida 14 - $1^{5}/_{8}$" x $1^{1}/_{2}$". Inserted in $2^{1}/_{2}$" square frame.
Santa Trimming Tree: Ivory Hardanger - $1^{1}/_{4}$" x $1^{1}/_{8}$". Inserted in $1^{3}/_{4}$" ring.
Train: Ivory Hardanger - 2" x $1^{1}/_{2}$". Inserted in wooden ornament.
Teddy Bear: Ivory Hardanger - $1^{3}/_{4}$" x $1^{5}/_{8}$". Inserted in $2^{1}/_{2}$" ring.
Madonna and Child: Ivory Hardanger over 2 threads - $2^{3}/_{8}$" x 3". Inserted in oval frame.
Candy Canes: Dk Green Hardanger - $1^{5}/_{8}$" x $1^{1}/_{2}$". For finishing, refer to Canning Jar Lid Finishing. Also White Aida 14 - $2^{1}/_{2}$" x $2^{3}/_{8}$". Inserted in wooden box.
Holly Wreath: Ivory Hardanger - $1^{3}/_{4}$" x $1^{7}/_{8}$". Inserted in $2\frac{1}{2}$" ring.
Candy Wreath: Ivory Hardanger - $1^{1}/_{2}$" x $1^{1}/_{2}$". Inserted in $2\frac{1}{2}$" square frame. Also Ivory Aida 18 - $1^{7}/_{8}$" x $1^{7}/_{8}$". For finishing, refer to Canning Jar Lid Finishing.
Stocking: Ivory Hardanger - $1^{1}/_{4}$" x $1^{5}/_{8}$". Inserted in $2^{1}/_{2}$" ring.
Large Blue Bells: Ivory Hardanger - $1^{3}/_{8}$" x $1^{1}/_{2}$". Inserted in $2^{1}/_{2}$" ring.
Candy Jar: Ivory Hardanger - $1^{5}/_{8}$" x $1^{1}/_{2}$". Inserted in $2^{1}/_{2}$" ring. Also White Hardanger - For finishing, refer to Canning Jar Lid Finishing.
Snowmen Carolers: Lt Blue Aida 14 - $2^{1}/_{2}$" x $2^{1}/_{2}$". Inserted in lucite box. Also Ivory Hardanger - $1^{5}/_{8}$" x $1^{5}/_{8}$". Inserted in wooden ornament.
Large Candle with Holly: Ivory Hardanger - $1^{1}/_{2}$" x $1^{5}/_{8}$". Inserted in $2^{1}/_{2}$" ring. Also Ivory Aida 14 - $2^{1}/_{4}$" x $2^{1}/_{2}$". Inserted in 3" frame.
Reindeer: Ivory Aida 18 - $2^{1}/_{8}$" x $2^{1}/_{8}$". Inserted in 3" ring.
Initial Square Design: White Aida 14 - $3^{1}/_{2}$" x $3^{1}/_{2}$". Inserted in lucite coaster. Refer to Alphabet on pg. 13 for personalization. Also White Aida 14 - Inserted in lucite paperweight.
Holiday Greetings: Dk Green Hardanger using white embroidery floss - $1^{3}/_{8}$" x $1^{3}/_{8}$". For finishing, refer to Button Ornament Finishing.
Merry Christmas: White Aida 14 - $3^{1}/_{2}$" x $3^{1}/_{2}$". Inserted in lucite coaster. Center of design on Red Aida 14 - 2" x 2". Inserted in wooden ornament.
Waiting For Santa: Ivory Aida 14 - $3^{1}/_{4}$" x $5^{1}/_{2}$". Inserted in 5" x 7" frame.
God Bless Santa Claus: Ivory Aida 14 - $3^{1}/_{4}$" x $5^{1}/_{2}$". Inserted in 5" x 7" frame.
Christmas Tree: White Hardanger over 2 threads - 1" x 1". Inserted in $1^{3}/_{4}$" ring.
Snowflake #1: Dk Blue Hardanger over 2 threads using white embroidery floss - $1^{3}/_{8}$" x $1^{3}/_{8}$". Inserted in $2^{1}/_{2}$" ring.
Small Wreath: Ivory Aida 14 - $1^{1}/_{8}$" x $1^{1}/_{8}$". Inserted in $1^{3}/_{4}$" ring.
Snowflake #2: White Aida 14 - $1^{1}/_{4}$" x $1^{1}/_{4}$". For finishing, refer to Button Ornament Finishing.
Mrs. Claus: Ivory Aida 14 - $1^{5}/_{8}$" x $1^{5}/_{8}$". Inserted in $2^{1}/_{2}$" ring.
Santa Claus #2: Ivory Aida 14 - 2" x $1^{3}/_{4}$". Inserted in $2^{1}/_{2}$" ring.
Small Gold Bells: Ivory Aida 14 - $1^{3}/_{8}$" x $1^{3}/_{8}$". Inserted in $2^{1}/_{2}$" ring. Also Ivory Hardanger - $^{7}/_{8}$" x $^{7}/_{8}$". Inserted in lucite picture holder.
Pump: Ivory Aida 14 - $3^{1}/_{8}$" x $3^{3}/_{4}$". Inserted In 4" x 5" frame.
Mailbox: Ivory Aida 14 - $3^{1}/_{4}$" x $3^{3}/_{4}$". Inserted in 4" x 5" frame.
Initial Round Design: Ivory Aida 14 - $2^{1}/_{2}$" x $2^{5}/_{8}$". Inserted in lucite coaster or glass paperweight. Refer to Alphabet on pg. 13 for personalization.